Mariska Hargitay's
Incredible Life Journey

INSIDE THE EXTRAORDINARY WORLD OF THE 'LAW AND ORDER: SVU' STAR

MARIA J. SHERMAN

COPYRIGHT © 2024 BY MARIA J. SHERMAN

No part of this book may be reproduced, duplicated, or transmitted in any form without the express written consent of the author or publisher. The author and publisher assume no legal responsibility or liability for any damages, losses, or other consequences resulting from the use or misuse of the information provided herein, whether directly or indirectly.

Legal Notices:

This book is protected under copyright law and is intended for personal use only. It is prohibited to modify, distribute, sell, quote, or paraphrase any part of this book without prior permission from the author or publisher.

Disclaimer:

This book is an independent publication and is not authorized, endorsed, or affiliated with Mariska Hargitay or her representatives. All trademarks, product names, and company names or logos mentioned herein are the property of their respective owners and are used for identification purposes only.

TABLE OF CONTENTS

INTRODUCTION   7

CHAPTER 1   14

A STAR IS BORN – GROWING UP IN THE SPOTLIGHT   14
TRAGEDY AND RESILIENCE   16
FINDING HER OWN PATH   17

CHAPTER 2   20

EARLY STRUGGLES AND BUILDING A CAREER   20
UCLA AND MISS BEVERLY HILLS USA   21
ENTERING THE WORLD OF HOLLYWOOD   22
MISSED OPPORTUNITIES AND MINOR SETBACKS   23
BREAKTHROUGH ROLES AND CONTINUED GROWTH   24
OVERCOMING CHALLENGES AND SHAPING HER FUTURE
    26

CHAPTER 3   28

THE ROLE OF A LIFETIME – OLIVIA BENSON ON LAW & ORDER: SVU — 28
CHARACTER DEVELOPMENT: THE EVOLUTION OF OLIVIA BENSON — 30
IMPACT ON THE PUBLIC: HOW OLIVIA BENSON RESONATED WITH FANS — 33

CHAPTER 4 — 37

THE SVU LEGACY — 37
MARISKA HARGITAY'S INFLUENCE ON REAL-WORLD SEXUAL ASSAULT AWARENESS AND ADVOCACY — 39
KEY EPISODES AND THEIR IMPACT ON FANS AND SOCIETY — 42

CHAPTER 5 — 45

ADVOCATE FOR CHANGE — 45
ADVOCACY FOR SURVIVORS OF SEXUAL VIOLENCE AND TRAUMA — 48
PUBLIC APPEARANCES, SPEECHES, AND THE FIGHT FOR JUSTICE REFORM — 51

CHAPTER 6 — 54

Balancing Family and Fame — 54
Raising Children While Maintaining a High-Profile Career — 56

CHAPTER 7 — 62

Awards and Accolades — 62
Industry Recognition and Her Influence as a TV Icon — 65
How Mariska Redefined the Role of Women in Television — 67

CHAPTER 8 — 71

Overcoming Personal Challenges — 71
Physical and Emotional Struggles Throughout Her Career — 71
Injuries on Set and Recovery — 73
Personal Stories of Resilience and Overcoming Adversity — 75

CHAPTER 9 77

BEYOND 'LAW & ORDER: SVU' – EXPLORING OTHER PROJECTS 77
FILM AND TV ROLES OUTSIDE OF 'SVU' 78
DIRECTORIAL AND PRODUCTION WORK 80
OTHER CREATIVE VENTURES 83

CHAPTER 10 85

MARISKA'S LASTING LEGACY 85
THE IMPACT OF HER CAREER ON TELEVISION AND SOCIETY 86
HOW MARISKA HARGITAY BECAME A SYMBOL OF STRENGTH AND JUSTICE 88

CONCLUSION 91

INTRODUCTION

Mariska Hargitay's life has been marked by profound loss, extraordinary resilience, and a relentless pursuit of justice—both on and off the screen. Born into Hollywood royalty on January 23, 1964, Mariska is the daughter of legendary actress Jayne Mansfield and bodybuilder Mickey Hargitay, a former Mr. Universe. Despite her glamorous beginnings, her early years were shaped by tragedy, one that would leave an indelible mark on her life and later inspire her work as an advocate for survivors of trauma.

On June 29, 1967, when Mariska was just three-and-a-half years old, her world was turned upside down. Her mother, Jayne Mansfield, was involved in a horrific car accident that claimed the lives of Mansfield, her boyfriend Sam Brody, and the driver. Mariska, along with her two older brothers, Miklós and Zoltán, were asleep in the backseat of the vehicle at the time of the accident. Miraculously, they survived, but the trauma of that night left Mariska with a lasting reminder in the form of a zigzag scar on one side of her head.

In interviews, Mariska has spoken candidly about how the loss of her mother left a deep emotional wound that would never fully heal. "I will always be a girl who lost her mom," she said, reflecting on the profound impact of growing up without Jayne Mansfield's larger-than-life presence. Raised by her father Mickey and his third wife, Ellen Siano, Mariska had to navigate the complexities of grief, fame, and growing up in the shadow of her famous parents.

Despite these challenges, Mariska forged her own path, determined not to be defined by her tragic past or her famous lineage. From a young age, she was keenly aware of the comparisons to her mother, a cultural icon whose beauty and bold personality captured the world's attention. But Mariska was determined to carve out her own identity, once remarking at age 18, "My dad was Mr. Universe, so it would be fun for me to be Miss Universe." This statement reflected her playful personality, but also her desire to be seen for who she truly was—a unique individual with her own dreams and aspirations.

Mariska's journey from the little girl who lost her mother to the television icon and advocate she is today is nothing short of extraordinary. It is a story of survival, strength, and self-discovery, shaped by personal challenges and triumphs alike. Her life has not only been defined by her illustrious acting career, most notably as Olivia Benson on Law & Order: Special Victims Unit, but also by her unwavering commitment to advocating for survivors of sexual assault, domestic violence, and child abuse.

In this book, we explore Mariska's incredible life journey, from her early days growing up in a household touched by tragedy to her rise as one of the most beloved figures in television history. We delve into her personal and professional challenges, her passion for justice, and the lasting impact she has made on both Hollywood and society. Through her groundbreaking role on SVU, Mariska Hargitay has become more than just an actress—she has become a symbol of strength, empathy, and resilience, inspiring millions around the world.

From the beginning, Mariska's life was intertwined with the complexities of fame. As the daughter of Jayne Mansfield, whose provocative persona and tragic death made her a tabloid fixture, Mariska had to navigate the pressures of living in the public eye. Yet, she chose a different route, one defined not by the glamour of Hollywood, but by her desire to connect with people on a deeper level. She knew that she did not want to be compared to her mother, saying, "I don't look at myself in the mirror and see her face; I see my own."

Her father's protective influence provided a sense of stability in a world that was anything but stable. Mickey Hargitay, a man who had built his career on physical strength, offered Mariska a foundation of emotional resilience. He helped her build her own identity, separate from the world of glamour that had enveloped her mother. Through his love and guidance, Mariska found the courage to embrace her own journey, which would ultimately lead her to the world of acting.

Mariska's entrance into the acting world was not a bid to follow in her mother's footsteps but rather a calling that grew from her own passion for storytelling. She started her career in the late 1980s, taking on small roles in television and film. Although she faced the inevitable comparisons to Jayne Mansfield, Mariska focused on honing her craft and finding roles that allowed her to showcase her range as an actress.

Her early career was marked by a series of guest appearances on popular television shows, but it wasn't until she landed the role of Olivia Benson on Law & Order: Special Victims Unit in 1999 that her life would change forever. Little did she know at the time that this role would not only define her career but also provide her with a platform to make a real difference in the world.

Portraying Olivia Benson would become Mariska's life work in many ways, but the role was more than just a job—it was a calling. As Benson, a detective who investigates sex crimes and fights tirelessly for victims, Mariska found herself deeply connected to the stories of survivors. She has often said that playing Benson made her more empathetic and aware of the real-world struggles faced by those who have experienced sexual violence.

Her portrayal of Benson resonated with viewers in ways that transcended the usual connection between actor and audience. Fans saw in Benson a beacon of hope, a champion for those who had been silenced. Through her work on SVU, Mariska helped to raise awareness about issues of sexual violence and abuse, making Olivia Benson not just a fictional character, but a symbol of strength and justice.

Mariska's dedication to advocacy didn't stop when the cameras stopped rolling. In 2004, she founded the Joyful Heart Foundation, an organization that supports survivors of sexual assault, domestic violence, and child abuse. Her work with Joyful Heart has expanded far beyond her role on SVU, positioning her as a real-world advocate for change. Through public appearances, speeches, and tireless activism, Mariska has used her platform to push for justice reform, raise awareness about the backlog of untested rape kits, and offer support to countless survivors.

CHAPTER 1

A Star is Born – Growing Up in the Spotlight

Mariska Hargitay was born on January 23, 1964, into a family steeped in Hollywood glamour and fame. Her mother, Jayne Mansfield, was a blonde bombshell who became one of the most iconic actresses of the 1950s and early 1960s, often compared to Marilyn Monroe for her beauty and sex appeal. Mansfield's career soared with her roles in films like Will Success Spoil Rock Hunter? and The Girl Can't Help It, making her a household name. Her magnetic presence in the entertainment industry was amplified by her personal life, which often made tabloid headlines. Mansfield's highly publicized relationships and extravagant lifestyle cemented her as a symbol of Hollywood excess, yet behind the glamorous facade, she was an intelligent woman with ambitions beyond acting.

Mariska's father, Mickey Hargitay, added another layer of fame and fortune to her lineage. Mickey was a Hungarian-born bodybuilder who won the title of Mr. Universe in 1955. He became a fixture in the entertainment world not only because of his successful bodybuilding career but also due to his marriage to Mansfield, making them one of Hollywood's most talked-about couples. Hargitay also dabbled in acting, most notably appearing alongside his wife in films like Promises! Promises! and The Loves of Hercules.

Mariska's parents had a profound impact on her life, shaping both the opportunities and challenges she would face growing up. From an early age, Mariska was immersed in the world of show business, often appearing in the media alongside her famous parents. Though her mother's fame was larger-than-life, the legacy she left was complex—one filled with glamour but also tumult. Growing up as the daughter of two celebrated figures, Mariska had to grapple with their fame, the expectations placed on her, and the attention that came with being a member of Hollywood royalty.

Tragedy and Resilience

Mariska's life took a tragic turn at a very young age. In 1967, when she was just three years old, her mother Jayne Mansfield was killed in a car accident, an event that shocked the entertainment world. The accident claimed Mansfield's life instantly, leaving behind her five children, including Mariska and her brothers, Zoltan and Mickey Jr., who were in the back seat of the car but miraculously survived.

The loss of her mother was devastating, and although Mariska was too young to fully understand the tragedy at the time, the impact it had on her life would be profound. She has often spoken about the emotional scars left by this early trauma, noting that the absence of her mother affected her deeply as she grew older. The car accident itself became a haunting symbol of the dangers of fame, but it also fostered in Mariska a remarkable resilience and strength. The world expected her to be the daughter of a bombshell icon, but she would eventually carve her own path, shaped by the loss and the lessons it brought her.

In the years following the accident, Mariska's father Mickey Hargitay took on the role of raising his children. He proved to be a loving and dedicated father, providing the stability and support that Mariska needed to heal from her loss. Mickey's discipline and work ethic, honed through his bodybuilding career, helped ground Mariska during difficult times, fostering in her a determination to rise above her challenges. She has often credited her father with teaching her how to stay strong, even when life throws its hardest punches. Through his example, Mariska learned the value of resilience, hard work, and the importance of family.

Finding Her Own Path

Growing up in the public eye, Mariska was constantly reminded of her parents' fame. Hollywood was her backdrop, and with that came the pressures of living up to the legacies of two larger-than-life figures. From a young age, Mariska was aware that people expected her to follow in her mother's footsteps, perhaps to become the next Jayne Mansfield. However, she was determined to forge her own identity, one that would honor her parents but be uniquely her own.

As a teenager, Mariska felt the weight of her mother's iconic image. Jayne Mansfield's sex symbol persona, while celebrated, was a challenging image for Mariska to contend with. She did not want to be confined to the stereotype of a glamorous Hollywood starlet, and the expectations surrounding her often felt suffocating. While she admired her mother's achievements, Mariska sought a different kind of success—one grounded in substance and depth.

Mariska navigated her childhood and adolescence with the guidance of her father and a strong sense of independence. She was drawn to the arts, studying acting at UCLA and later attending the prestigious Groundlings Theater and School in Los Angeles. This pursuit helped Mariska develop her own voice as a performer, outside of her mother's shadow. She was determined to be taken seriously as an actress, and her early experiences in school and on stage gave her the tools to do so.

Despite her famous last name, Mariska experienced the same struggles as many aspiring actors. She went on auditions, faced rejection, and had to prove her talent in an industry that often made assumptions about her based on her family. But Mariska's dedication and perseverance paid off. By the time she was in her twenties, she had begun landing small roles in film and television, slowly building her career from the ground up.

Though she carried the legacy of her parents, Mariska Hargitay was set on creating a career that was defined by her own accomplishments, not by the fame of those who came before her. She learned how to embrace her roots while also stepping out from the shadows, evolving into the celebrated actress and advocate the world would come to know. This journey of self-discovery and determination would serve as the foundation for the career that awaited her—a career defined by hard work, authenticity, and a desire to make a difference.

CHAPTER 2

Early Struggles and Building a Career

High School Years and Early Interests

Mariska Hargitay's passion for the arts began to take shape during her time at Marymount High School, a Catholic secondary school in Los Angeles. Though she was the daughter of two Hollywood stars, Mariska did not initially see herself following in their footsteps. At Marymount, she immersed herself in various activities, displaying a well-rounded set of interests that extended beyond acting. She actively participated in cheerleading, student government, athletics, and the school's theater program. Each of these roles helped cultivate her leadership skills, confidence, and stage presence, but it was acting that truly captured her heart.

Her time in the theater program at Marymount laid the groundwork for her eventual pursuit of acting as a career. Mariska thrived in the structured environment of the school's productions, and it was here that she began to realize that performing was not just a pastime but a passion she wanted to turn into a profession. These formative experiences during her teenage years gave her the foundation to navigate the entertainment industry in her future endeavors.

UCLA and Miss Beverly Hills USA

After graduating from high school in 1982, Mariska enrolled at the University of California, Los Angeles (UCLA), where she pursued a degree in theater at the School of Theater, Film, and Television. She also joined the Kappa Kappa Gamma sorority, finding a supportive community that balanced her academic and personal growth. Although she left UCLA before completing her degree, the experience allowed her to hone her acting skills and build relationships with like-minded students who shared her passion for the craft.

The same year she started at UCLA, Mariska added another achievement to her resume: she was crowned Miss Beverly Hills USA, which set her on a new trajectory. Competing in beauty pageants was a common stepping stone for many aspiring actresses in the 1980s, and for Mariska, it provided an opportunity to gain exposure. Her win in the Beverly Hills competition was followed by participation in the Miss California USA pageant, where she placed fourth runner-up. Although she didn't win the state crown, her participation further cemented her determination to pursue a career in the spotlight.

Entering the World of Hollywood

By the time she was a freshman in college, Mariska had already secured an agent and began landing small roles in television and film. In 1984, she appeared in the music video for country singer Ronnie Milsap's hit song "She Loves My Car," making it the first country music video to air on MTV. While it was a small step, it marked her entrance into the entertainment world, allowing her to demonstrate her versatility. The following year, she landed her first film role in the low-budget horror flick Ghoulies (1985). Though the movie didn't garner much critical acclaim, it was Mariska's first opportunity to appear on the big screen, signaling the start of her acting journey.

Throughout the late 1980s and 1990s, Mariska appeared in a variety of television shows and films, building her resume brick by brick. She landed small roles in popular TV programs such as Freddy's Nightmares: A Nightmare on Elm Street: The Series, Baywatch, and thirtysomething. In the 1988 hit prime-time soap opera Falcon Crest, Mariska secured a recurring role as Carly Fixx, which marked a significant turning point in her career. The role gave her more exposure, and she began to establish herself as a working actor in Hollywood, no longer defined solely by her famous lineage.

Missed Opportunities and Minor Setbacks

Despite these early successes, Mariska Hargitay's career path was not without its share of challenges. In the late 1980s, she was briefly cast as Dulcea in Mighty Morphin Power Rangers: The Movie, only for her scenes to be cut when the original actress recovered from surgery and returned to the role. While this may have been a frustrating experience for a young actress on the rise, Mariska remained undeterred.

Her early career was filled with moments like these—where opportunities were gained and lost—but each setback became a lesson in resilience and determination. Mariska also experienced frequent comparisons to her late mother, Jayne Mansfield. Although she admired her mother's legacy, Mariska found the constant comparisons to be challenging, especially as she wanted to be recognized for her own talents and hard work, not just as "Jayne Mansfield's daughter." She worked diligently to separate her career from her mother's iconic status, determined to be known for her own acting achievements.

Breakthrough Roles and Continued Growth

In 1992, Mariska was cast as Officer Angela Garcia in the action-comedy TV series Tequila and Bonetti. Though the series only lasted one season, Mariska's role as a police officer proved to be a harbinger of her future career-defining role on Law & Order: SVU. It was here that she began to explore the complexities of playing a law enforcement character, unknowingly preparing herself for the part that would change her life years later.

In the mid-1990s, Mariska continued to appear in various television roles. She played Didi Edelstein, the sultry next-door neighbor in the sitcom Can't Hurry Love, which showcased her ability to handle both comedic and dramatic roles. Additionally, she portrayed Detective Nina Echeverria in the short-lived crime drama Prince Street in 1997. Though many of these roles were minor or in short-lived series, they were crucial stepping stones that allowed Mariska to develop her craft and gain more visibility in the competitive world of Hollywood.

Perhaps one of her most memorable minor roles during this period came when she guest-starred on the two-part fourth season finale of Seinfeld. In the episode titled "The Pilot," Mariska's character reads for the role of Elaine Benes, which provided her with a comedic moment that endeared her to a new audience. This appearance, though brief, allowed her to showcase her versatility as an actress capable of handling different genres.

Overcoming Challenges and Shaping Her Future

As Mariska navigated the ups and downs of her early career, she faced the same challenges that many aspiring actors face—constant auditions, rejections, and the need to prove herself in an industry that can be unforgiving. While she experienced moments of frustration, especially with roles that didn't pan out or projects that didn't find success, she remained focused on her ultimate goal: to build a sustainable career in acting.

By the mid-1990s, she had appeared on an impressive roster of TV shows, including ER, where she played desk clerk Cynthia Hooper, and Freddy's Nightmares, a TV spin-off of the popular Nightmare on Elm Street film franchise. Though many of these roles were smaller parts, they each provided invaluable experience and continued to bolster her growing resume.

Mariska's perseverance through these early years would ultimately lead to the breakthrough role that she had worked so hard for—a role that would not only define her career but also change the trajectory of her life. However, before that moment arrived, Mariska had to endure years of hard work, minor successes, and the inevitable setbacks that come with trying to make a name for oneself in Hollywood.

In the end, Mariska Hargitay's early struggles and her dedication to the craft of acting laid the foundation for the success that would follow. Each role, no matter how small, became a stepping stone toward the career-defining moment that would come when she stepped into the shoes of Olivia Benson on Law & Order: Special Victims Unit. But the journey to that point was one of resilience, hard work, and a commitment to proving herself as more than just a Hollywood legacy—Mariska Hargitay was destined to be a star in her own right.

CHAPTER 3

The Role of a Lifetime – Olivia Benson on Law & Order: SVU

Mariska Hargitay's journey to becoming Detective Olivia Benson on Law & Order: Special Victims Unit (SVU) was one marked by timing, perseverance, and the culmination of years of hard work. By the late 1990s, Hargitay had spent over a decade steadily building her career, taking on minor roles in television shows and films. However, she had not yet secured the breakthrough part that would truly define her acting career. That moment came in 1999, when she auditioned for the lead role of Olivia Benson in a new crime drama series from the Law & Order franchise that would focus on sexually based crimes.

At the time, Law & Order was already an immensely popular procedural drama, known for its gritty realism and focus on the criminal justice system. When creator Dick Wolf decided to develop a spin-off centered around the Special Victims Unit (SVU) of the New York Police

Department, it was a bold move, given that the show would deal with sensitive and often harrowing subjects, such as sexual assault, child abuse, and domestic violence. The character of Olivia Benson, a compassionate and driven detective, was envisioned as the moral compass of the show—someone who would bring both strength and empathy to her work.

Hargitay's initial interest in the role came from the compelling nature of the script. Olivia Benson was a character unlike any she had encountered in her previous work. The character's backstory, as a child born from her mother's rape, immediately gave Benson a deep connection to the cases she would investigate, making her not only a skilled detective but someone who personally understood the trauma her victims experienced. Hargitay felt an almost immediate bond with Benson and knew this was the role she had been waiting for.

Mariska Hargitay's audition for the part was a pivotal moment. Christopher Meloni, who had already been cast as her co-star and partner, Detective Elliot Stabler, was in the room for her screen test. The chemistry between the two actors was palpable, and their dynamic would go on to be one of the central elements of the show's early success. Hargitay later recounted how she felt an instant connection with Meloni, and how their different acting styles complemented one another—his intensity balancing her emotional depth. This chemistry, coupled with Hargitay's natural ability to convey vulnerability and strength, secured her the role.

After landing the part, Hargitay immersed herself in research to fully understand the reality of working in a special victims unit. She underwent training with police officers, rode along with real-life detectives, and spoke with survivors of sexual violence. This preparation not only informed her portrayal of Benson but also deepened her understanding of the real-world impact her character could have.

Character Development: The Evolution of Olivia Benson

Over the years, Olivia Benson has grown into one of the most iconic characters in television history, and much of that evolution is due to Mariska Hargitay's input into the role. From the beginning, Benson was portrayed as a compassionate, empathetic detective with an unyielding commitment to seeking justice for survivors. As the series progressed, so too did Benson's depth and complexity, as she dealt with personal and professional challenges that shaped her into the formidable figure she is today.

In the early seasons of SVU, Benson's character was deeply tied to her partnership with Detective Elliot Stabler. Their relationship, though not romantic, was one of the strongest on television, defined by mutual respect, loyalty, and the intensity with which they approached their work. Stabler's more aggressive and emotionally volatile nature was often balanced by Benson's empathy and level-headedness. Together, they navigated some of the darkest aspects of human behavior, forming a partnership that captivated audiences and became a central element of the show's success.

As the series progressed, however, Hargitay and the showrunners worked to develop Benson beyond her role as Stabler's partner. Following Meloni's departure from the show in 2011, Benson's character was thrust into new territory, and the focus shifted more heavily onto her individual journey. Hargitay welcomed the opportunity to explore different aspects of Benson's personality, including her vulnerabilities, her longing for a family, and her struggles with balancing her personal life and career.

One of the key turning points in Benson's evolution was her eventual promotion to Sergeant and later Lieutenant, becoming the commanding officer of the Special Victims Unit. This role came with significant responsibility, and Hargitay relished the chance to portray Benson's growth as a leader. No longer just investigating cases, Benson was now in charge of making tough decisions, mentoring her detectives, and continuing to fight for justice while navigating the pressures of leadership. Hargitay's portrayal of Benson's internal conflict—whether she could still be the compassionate detective she once was while carrying the weight of command—added new layers to the character.

Another major development in Benson's arc was her decision to become a mother. The adoption of her son,

Noah, allowed the audience to see a more personal side of Benson as she navigated single motherhood while continuing to work in a high-stakes, emotionally draining job. Hargitay infused Benson's relationship with Noah with warmth, vulnerability, and fierce protectiveness, further deepening the character's relatability and complexity.

Hargitay has been very vocal about how much personal input she has had into Benson's development over the years. As both an actress and a producer on the show, Hargitay has had a significant say in the direction her character has taken. She has advocated for storylines that reflect the realities of sexual assault survivors and has worked closely with the show's writers to ensure that Benson's journey remains true to the character's mission of seeking justice and supporting victims.

Impact on the Public: How Olivia Benson Resonated with Fans

Perhaps the most profound aspect of Mariska Hargitay's portrayal of Olivia Benson is the impact the character has had on audiences, particularly survivors of sexual violence. From the very beginning, Law & Order: SVU has been lauded for its sensitive and nuanced portrayal of crimes that are often difficult to talk about. At the heart of the show's mission is a dedication to giving voice to survivors, and no character embodies that more than Olivia Benson.

Benson's empathy, resilience, and unwavering commitment to her work have made her a beacon of hope for many viewers. For survivors of sexual violence, in particular, Benson has become a symbol of strength and validation. Mariska Hargitay has often spoken about the letters she receives from fans who have shared their personal stories of trauma, abuse, and survival. Many of these letters express how Benson's character has helped them feel seen, heard, and empowered to seek justice or healing.

Hargitay's connection to the cause of supporting survivors extends far beyond her portrayal of Benson on screen. In 2004, she founded the Joyful Heart Foundation, a nonprofit organization dedicated to helping survivors of sexual assault, domestic violence, and child abuse. The foundation provides resources, support, and advocacy for survivors, and has been instrumental in raising awareness about issues related to sexual violence. Through her work with the foundation, Hargitay has become a real-life advocate for the same causes her character fights for on SVU.

Benson's impact on the public is also reflected in how the character has broken down barriers in terms of representation. As a female detective in a male-dominated field, Benson has shattered stereotypes and proven that women in law enforcement can be just as tough, effective, and capable as their male counterparts. Her ability to balance strength with compassion has made her a role model for both women and men in real-life law enforcement and beyond.

The longevity of SVU—now the longest-running primetime live-action series in American television history—speaks to the resonance of the show and the character of Olivia Benson. Over the years, Benson has become more than just a fictional detective; she is a cultural icon and a symbol of justice, empathy, and strength.

CHAPTER 4

The SVU Legacy

Law & Order: Special Victims Unit (SVU) has left an indelible mark on television, society, and the way we address the complex issues surrounding sexual violence. When it premiered in 1999, few could have predicted that it would become the longest-running primetime live-action television series in American history. With more than 25 seasons and over 500 episodes, SVU transcended its status as a mere procedural drama to become a cultural phenomenon, influencing public discourse on topics like sexual assault, consent, and the treatment of victims in both legal and social contexts.

The show's cultural resonance is largely due to its willingness to explore difficult and often taboo subjects. By focusing on sexually based offenses, SVU brought attention to crimes that had historically been underrepresented in media. These episodes, often "ripped from the headlines," struck a chord with viewers by reflecting real-world events and highlighting systemic failures in how sexual violence is addressed. In doing so, SVU became more than entertainment—it became a vital platform for educating viewers about these complex issues and pushing the conversation forward.

SVU stood out from its parent show, Law & Order, by humanizing its victims and providing a more emotional, psychological portrayal of trauma. The show not only detailed the meticulous police work and courtroom procedures required to bring perpetrators to justice but also delved into the personal toll these crimes took on survivors. This dual focus on law enforcement and victim advocacy made the show a unique bridge between entertainment and social awareness.

Part of the show's lasting appeal is its ability to adapt to evolving cultural norms and discussions. Over its long tenure, SVU has reflected shifts in society's understanding of sexual violence, consent, gender dynamics, and power imbalances. From addressing celebrity sexual assault scandals to exploring the impact of movements like #MeToo, SVU has remained culturally relevant, continually adapting its storytelling to mirror the world around it. As social consciousness grew, so did the complexity of the cases tackled on the show, resulting in episodes that not only entertained but also educated and raised awareness.

SVU has also influenced other crime dramas and television shows. Its success demonstrated that there was an appetite for crime dramas that deal with sensitive, emotional, and challenging topics. Shows like Criminal Minds, Chicago P.D., and NCIS have incorporated elements of SVU's approach to victim-focused storytelling. The longevity of SVU is a testament to its enduring relevance and its ability to continue captivating new generations of viewers.

Mariska Hargitay's Influence on Real-World Sexual Assault Awareness and Advocacy

At the heart of SVU's success is Mariska Hargitay and her iconic portrayal of Detective Olivia Benson, later Captain, and head of the Special Victims Unit. From the moment

Hargitay stepped into the role, she brought a depth and emotional authenticity to Benson that resonated with viewers, particularly survivors of sexual violence. Benson's character is compassionate, fierce, and unwavering in her pursuit of justice for victims. Her empathy and understanding towards survivors, combined with her no-nonsense approach to law enforcement, made her a beloved and respected figure.

However, Hargitay's influence extends far beyond the screen. The sheer volume of letters and personal stories from survivors that Hargitay received after portraying Benson led her to realize the real-world impact her character was having. These survivors were not just thanking Hargitay for her performance—they were sharing their experiences, seeking support, and finding validation through Benson's character. This profound connection with viewers inspired Hargitay to take action in a way that few actors have ever done.

In 2004, Hargitay founded the Joyful Heart Foundation, a nonprofit organization dedicated to supporting survivors of sexual assault, domestic violence, and child abuse. The foundation's mission is to transform society's response to these forms of violence, support survivors' healing, and end this violence once and for all. Through the foundation, Hargitay has advocated for the rights of survivors, raised awareness about the backlog of untested rape kits in the United States, and worked tirelessly to change laws and policies related to sexual violence.

Hargitay's advocacy has not only made a difference in the lives of survivors but also transformed the conversation around sexual violence. She has testified before Congress, partnered with lawmakers and organizations, and worked on numerous public service campaigns. Her advocacy directly influenced the passage of legislation, including the Sexual Assault Survivors' Rights Act, which was signed into law in 2016. Her efforts have empowered countless survivors to come forward, find their voice, and seek justice.

In many ways, Hargitay's off-screen work mirrors the resilience and dedication of her on-screen persona. Olivia Benson is not just a fictional character—through

Hargitay's real-world efforts, she has become a symbol of hope, advocacy, and justice for survivors everywhere.

Key Episodes and Their Impact on Fans and Society

Throughout its long run, SVU has delivered several key episodes that have resonated deeply with fans and society at large. These episodes not only reflect important social issues but have also sparked real-world conversations and change.

"Loss" (Season 5, Episode 4): In this episode, Benson and Stabler investigate a sex trafficking ring that targets young girls. This episode highlighted the horrors of human trafficking, an issue that many viewers were unaware of at the time. The episode's emotional depth and depiction of victims as real, complex individuals left a lasting impression on audiences and raised awareness about modern-day slavery.

"911" (Season 7, Episode 3): This Emmy-winning episode focuses on a frantic race to save a young girl, who is being held captive, after she calls 911. The entire episode takes place with Benson on the phone with the child, showcasing Hargitay's emotional range and highlighting the vulnerability of child victims. The episode won critical acclaim and is often cited as one of the most intense and impactful in the show's history.

"Undercover" (Season 9, Episode 15): Benson goes undercover in a women's prison to investigate the rape of an inmate. The episode addresses systemic sexual abuse within institutions, shedding light on an issue rarely discussed in mainstream media. It served as a wake-up call to many viewers about the abuse that can occur in places of supposed safety, prompting discussions about the treatment of prisoners and the importance of accountability.

"Surrender Benson" (Season 15, Episode 1): This harrowing episode follows Benson as she is kidnapped and tortured by a serial rapist she had been investigating. The episode is notable for its unflinching portrayal of trauma and recovery, and it gave Hargitay the opportunity to portray Benson's vulnerability and strength in the aftermath of her ordeal. This episode resonated with survivors of trauma, as it realistically depicted the emotional and psychological toll of such an experience.

"Theatre Tricks" (Season 13, Episode 11): This episode addresses the rise of digital and social media-related sexual violence, including cyberstalking and the non-consensual distribution of intimate images. It speaks to the modern landscape of sexual exploitation and the legal challenges of addressing crimes committed online. The episode's focus on emerging forms of sexual violence helped raise awareness about the dangers of technology in the wrong hands.

CHAPTER 5

Advocate for Change

Mariska's Work with the Joyful Heart Foundation

Mariska Hargitay's journey from television star to a passionate advocate for survivors of sexual violence is one of profound transformation. While her role as Olivia Benson on Law & Order: Special Victims Unit (SVU) introduced her to the traumatic experiences of survivors, it was the real-world stories shared by viewers that pushed Hargitay to take action beyond the screen. The emotional letters she received from fans, many of whom were survivors of sexual assault, domestic violence, and child abuse, sparked a sense of responsibility in her. Hargitay recognized that survivors were finding solace and empowerment in her portrayal of Benson, but they needed more than a fictional hero—they needed tangible support, advocacy, and resources.

In 2004, Hargitay founded the Joyful Heart Foundation, an organization dedicated to transforming society's response to sexual assault, domestic violence, and child abuse. What began as a vision to create a supportive community for survivors evolved into a national movement aimed at breaking the silence surrounding these forms of violence and promoting healing and justice. The foundation's mission is threefold: to heal, to educate, and to empower.

Healing is at the core of the Joyful Heart Foundation's work. The organization provides survivors with access to therapeutic services and programs that facilitate emotional and psychological recovery. Through retreats, wellness programs, and survivor support networks, Joyful Heart fosters a space where survivors can feel safe, understood, and heard. The foundation emphasizes holistic healing, focusing on the mind, body, and spirit to help survivors reclaim their lives. This approach reflects Hargitay's belief that true healing goes beyond physical recovery—it requires addressing the deep emotional scars left by trauma.

Education is another pillar of the foundation's mission. Joyful Heart has worked tirelessly to change the conversation around sexual violence, domestic abuse, and child exploitation. By raising awareness and providing training to professionals in law enforcement, healthcare, and social services, the organization seeks to improve how survivors are treated from the moment they report an incident. Hargitay's foundation has partnered with institutions across the country to educate the public on issues like consent, trauma-informed care, and the long-lasting effects of abuse. The foundation also provides educational resources for survivors, helping them navigate the legal system and access the services they need.

Finally, empowerment is central to everything Joyful Heart does. The organization not only advocates for survivors but also gives them a platform to tell their stories. By empowering survivors to speak out and reclaim their narratives, Joyful Heart helps dismantle the shame and stigma that often accompany experiences of sexual violence. This empowerment extends to legislative advocacy, as the foundation has been instrumental in pushing for systemic change in how the criminal justice system handles sexual assault cases.

Advocacy for Survivors of Sexual Violence and Trauma

Mariska Hargitay's advocacy work has had a transformative impact on the lives of countless survivors. Her efforts extend far beyond the Joyful Heart Foundation, as she has become a leading voice in the fight for justice reform and the fair treatment of survivors within the legal system.

One of the most significant areas of Hargitay's advocacy has been her work to eliminate the rape kit backlog. Across the United States, tens of thousands of untested rape kits—containing crucial DNA evidence—sat in storage for years, delaying justice for survivors and allowing perpetrators to escape accountability. The existence of this backlog highlighted a systemic failure in how sexual assault cases were handled, with many victims feeling forgotten by the system that was supposed to protect them.

Through the Joyful Heart Foundation's End the Backlog initiative, Hargitay spearheaded efforts to raise awareness of the issue and push for legislative reforms. She lobbied for funding to test these backlogged kits, collaborated with law enforcement agencies to improve the processing of forensic evidence, and worked with legislators to pass laws requiring the timely testing of rape kits. Thanks to her tireless advocacy, states across the country have implemented reforms to ensure that survivors are no longer left waiting for justice. In New York, for example, the passage of legislation mandating the prompt testing of rape kits was a direct result of Hargitay's influence.

Hargitay has also been a staunch advocate for trauma-informed care, which emphasizes the importance of treating survivors with empathy and understanding. Trauma-informed care requires professionals in law enforcement, healthcare, and social services to approach survivors with sensitivity to the emotional and psychological impact of trauma. Hargitay's foundation has provided training and resources to ensure that first responders and professionals who interact with survivors do so in a way that supports their recovery rather than retraumatizing them.

Through her advocacy, Hargitay has also shed light on the importance of mental health support for survivors. She has highlighted the long-term psychological effects of sexual violence, such as depression, anxiety, and PTSD, and has worked to make mental health services more accessible to survivors. Her work emphasizes that healing is not a linear process, and survivors need ongoing support to rebuild their lives after trauma.

Hargitay's commitment to survivors extends to advocating for legislative reforms that protect victims and hold perpetrators accountable. She has worked with lawmakers to pass bills that strengthen the rights of survivors, improve the handling of sexual assault cases, and increase funding for victim support services. Her efforts have contributed to landmark legislation, including the Sexual Assault Survivors' Rights Act, which grants survivors more control over their rape kits and ensures they have access to crucial information throughout the investigative process.

Public Appearances, Speeches, and the Fight for Justice Reform

Mariska Hargitay's advocacy has taken her to the halls of Congress, the stages of national conferences, and the platforms of global media. She has used her celebrity status to amplify the voices of survivors and to push for meaningful change in the justice system.

One of her most impactful public appearances came in 2016 when Hargitay testified before Congress about the rape kit backlog. In an emotional testimony, she shared stories from survivors who had been failed by the system and called for federal action to address the backlog. Her testimony helped bring national attention to the issue and contributed to the passage of federal funding measures aimed at reducing the backlog.

Hargitay has also been a frequent speaker at events dedicated to ending sexual violence and supporting survivors. At the United State of Women Summit, she spoke passionately about the need for society to take sexual violence seriously and to support survivors in their healing journeys. Her speeches are often a powerful blend of personal stories, survivor narratives, and calls to action, inspiring audiences to join the fight for justice.

Her public appearances are not limited to advocacy conferences. Hargitay has used her platform at awards shows, talk shows, and charity galas to speak out about the importance of survivor support. Whether accepting an award or sitting for an interview, she consistently redirects the spotlight to the cause of ending sexual violence and supporting those affected by it. In doing so, she has helped change the way the media discusses these issues, moving the conversation away from victim-blaming and toward a focus on accountability and healing.

In addition to her advocacy on the national stage, Hargitay has participated in grassroots efforts to support survivors. She has visited rape crisis centers, met with survivors, and engaged in local campaigns to raise awareness about sexual violence. Her hands-on approach demonstrates her deep commitment to the cause and her understanding that real change happens both on the ground and in the corridors of power.

Through her work with the Joyful Heart Foundation, her advocacy for justice reform, and her public appearances, Mariska Hargitay has become an indispensable voice in the fight against sexual violence. Her dedication to the cause has made her not just an actor portraying a hero on television, but a real-life advocate for survivors and a powerful agent of change.

CHAPTER 6

Balancing Family and Fame

In the world of Hollywood, balancing the demands of a high-profile career with personal relationships can be a challenge, but for Mariska Hargitay, her marriage to actor Peter Hermann has proven to be a source of strength and stability. The two actors first met in 2001 on the set of Law & Order: Special Victims Unit (SVU), where Hermann had a recurring role as defense attorney Trevor Langan. Their on-screen connection soon blossomed into an off-screen romance, marking the beginning of a relationship that would endure through the pressures of fame, family, and the demanding schedules of their respective careers.

Hargitay and Hermann's love story is a testament to the power of shared values and mutual respect. In interviews, Hargitay has often spoken about the immediate connection she felt with Hermann, who shared her strong commitment to family and faith. For Hargitay, this bond was deepened by Hermann's presence in her life during a pivotal time in her career, as SVU had begun to gain widespread popularity. While her career was reaching new heights, she found a partner in Hermann who not only understood the demands of the entertainment industry but also valued the importance of building a life together away from the public eye.

The couple married on August 28, 2004, in an intimate ceremony in Santa Barbara, California. The picturesque location and close-knit gathering of family and friends reflected Hargitay and Hermann's desire to keep their personal lives private and grounded, despite their growing fame. Their wedding day marked the start of a union that would remain strong in the face of the challenges that come with maintaining high-profile careers. For Hargitay, marrying Hermann was not just about finding a life partner; it was about building a family, a dream she had long cherished.

Raising Children While Maintaining a High-Profile Career

The arrival of children into their lives brought new joys and responsibilities for Hargitay and Hermann. On June 28, 2006, the couple welcomed their first child, a son named August, into the world. The birth was not without complications, as Hargitay underwent an emergency caesarean section, a difficult experience that further deepened her appreciation for the role of motherhood. Despite the demands of her role on SVU, Hargitay took on the challenges of motherhood with the same passion and commitment that she brought to her career. She has often said that becoming a mother changed her life in profound ways, giving her a new perspective on both her work and her personal life.

As a working mother, Hargitay faced the difficult task of balancing her career with the demands of raising a child. SVU had become one of the most-watched shows on television, and Hargitay's portrayal of Olivia Benson had cemented her as a household name. However, behind the scenes, she was navigating the challenges that many working mothers face: the constant juggling of responsibilities, the emotional pull between work and family, and the desire to be present for her child while continuing to pursue her professional ambitions.

Despite these challenges, Hargitay found ways to balance her dual roles. She has often spoken about the importance of setting boundaries and prioritizing time with her family, even when the demands of her career were at their peak. The support of her husband, Peter Hermann, was crucial during this time. Hermann, an actor with his own successful career, understood the pressures that came with Hargitay's role on SVU and provided unwavering support as they navigated parenthood together. Their partnership allowed Hargitay to continue pursuing her career while also being the kind of mother she aspired to be.

In April 2011, Hargitay and Hermann expanded their family when they adopted a baby girl named Amaya. The couple had long expressed their desire to adopt, and the arrival of Amaya was a joyful moment for the entire family. Hargitay and Hermann were present for Amaya's birth, and the experience of adopting a child was deeply meaningful for both of them. Hargitay has spoken about how adoption opened her heart in new ways and how Amaya's arrival brought immense joy and fulfillment to their lives. For Hargitay, becoming a mother to Amaya was a natural extension of her role as a parent, and she embraced the opportunity to provide a loving home for another child.

Later that same year, in October 2011, Hargitay and Hermann adopted a second son, Andrew, who had been born earlier in 2011. The decision to adopt two children within such a short period was a reflection of the couple's deep commitment to building a family that was full of love and support. Raising three children while maintaining a high-profile career was no easy feat, but for Hargitay, the rewards far outweighed the challenges. She has often described her family as her greatest achievement and her children as the center of her world.

The decision to adopt also reflected Hargitay's strong sense of empathy and her desire to create a loving, inclusive family. As the daughter of actress Jayne

Mansfield, who died when Hargitay was only three years old, Hargitay understood the importance of providing a stable and supportive home for her children. She has often spoken about how her own experiences with loss and resilience have shaped her approach to motherhood and family life. For Hargitay, being a mother is not just about biological connection; it is about love, care, and the ability to provide a nurturing environment for her children to thrive.

Hargitay's ability to balance her family life with her career is down to her resilience and dedication. Even as SVU continued to break records and Hargitay's portrayal of Olivia Benson earned her critical acclaim, she remained committed to being present for her family. In interviews, she has emphasized the importance of carving out time for her children, whether it's reading them bedtime stories, attending their school events, or simply being there for the everyday moments that make up a child's life.

Despite the long hours and intense demands of filming SVU, Hargitay has found ways to make her family a priority. She has spoken about the importance of having a strong support system, both at home and at work. The flexibility and understanding of her colleagues on SVU, combined with the support of Hermann, have allowed her to maintain a balance between her personal and professional life. Hargitay has often credited her husband with being a true partner in every sense of the word, describing him as her rock and the glue that holds their family together.

The couple's shared commitment to their children has been evident in their approach to parenting. Both Hargitay and Hermann have made it clear that family comes first, and they have worked together to create a stable and loving home for their children. They have also been open about the challenges of raising children in the public eye and the importance of maintaining a sense of normalcy for their family, despite their high-profile careers.

Hargitay's ability to balance family and fame has not gone unnoticed. She has often been hailed as a role model for working mothers, demonstrating that it is possible to pursue a successful career while also being a devoted parent. Her story is one of resilience, love, and the determination to create a fulfilling life both on and off the screen.

CHAPTER 7

Awards and Accolades

Mariska Hargitay's portrayal of Olivia Benson on Law & Order: Special Victims Unit (SVU) has become one of the most iconic performances in television history. From the moment she first stepped into the role in 1999, Hargitay's performance was met with widespread acclaim from critics and audiences alike. Her nuanced and empathetic portrayal of Benson, a detective (later Captain) in the NYPD's Special Victims Unit, resonated deeply with viewers. Hargitay was able to bring humanity and depth to the role, turning Benson into a symbol of strength, resilience, and compassion. Over the years, this performance has earned Hargitay numerous awards and accolades, solidifying her status as a television icon.

Hargitay's first major recognition for her work on SVU came in 2006 when she won the Primetime Emmy Award for Outstanding Lead Actress in a Drama Series. This victory was particularly significant because it marked the first time a performer from the Law & Order franchise had won an Emmy. Hargitay's win was a testament to the power of her portrayal and the emotional depth she brought to the character of Olivia Benson. In her acceptance speech, Hargitay dedicated the award to survivors of sexual violence, highlighting the connection she felt to her character's mission and the real-life issues the show addresses. This Emmy win was just the beginning of Hargitay's award recognition, as her portrayal of Benson would continue to garner critical acclaim throughout the years.

In addition to the Emmy, Hargitay has received numerous other prestigious awards for her role on SVU. In 2005, she won a Golden Globe Award for Best Actress in a Television Drama, further cementing her status as one of the most celebrated actresses in the industry. The Golden Globe win was particularly meaningful for Hargitay, as it recognized her ability to balance the emotional weight of the show's subject matter with the complexities of her character's personal journey. Her performance as Olivia Benson was not just about solving crimes; it was about showing the human cost of sexual violence and the toll it takes on both the victims and those who work to bring justice.

Throughout her career on SVU, Hargitay has been nominated for numerous other awards, including Screen Actors Guild Awards, People's Choice Awards, and Women's Image Network Awards. Each nomination and win has been a reflection of the widespread admiration for her portrayal of Benson and her ability to bring authenticity to the role. One of the reasons Hargitay's performance has resonated so deeply with audiences is her commitment to portraying Benson as a multifaceted character. Benson is tough, yet vulnerable; compassionate, yet relentless in her pursuit of justice. Hargitay's ability to capture these contradictions has made her one of the most beloved and respected actresses on television.

Industry Recognition and Her Influence as a TV Icon

Beyond the awards and critical acclaim, Mariska Hargitay's role on SVU has earned her a special place in the television industry as a trailblazer and a role model. Hargitay's portrayal of Olivia Benson has not only made her a household name but has also elevated her to the status of a TV icon. As the longest-running female character in prime-time television history, Hargitay has redefined what it means to be a leading woman in television. She has proven that a female character can be both powerful and empathetic, complex and relatable, and can carry a show for over two decades with consistency and grace.

Hargitay's influence extends beyond her acting. As SVU gained popularity, Hargitay became increasingly involved in shaping her character and influencing the direction of the show. Over the years, she has taken on a more active role behind the scenes, serving as an executive producer on SVU and contributing to the development of storylines and character arcs. Her leadership on set has been widely praised by her colleagues, who often speak of her dedication to her craft and her commitment to telling stories that matter.

As a television icon, Hargitay has also used her platform to advocate for important social issues. Inspired by her work on SVU and the stories of survivors of sexual violence, Hargitay founded the Joyful Heart Foundation in 2004. The foundation is dedicated to helping survivors of sexual assault, domestic violence, and child abuse heal and reclaim their lives. Through her advocacy work, Hargitay has raised awareness about the issues portrayed on SVU and has worked to change the way society responds to these crimes. Her activism has earned her recognition beyond the entertainment industry, and she has been honored with various humanitarian awards for her efforts.

Hargitay's influence as a TV icon is also evident in the way she has inspired a new generation of actresses and viewers. Olivia Benson has become a symbol of female empowerment, and Hargitay's portrayal has shown that women can be leaders, protectors, and change-makers. Young women who grew up watching SVU have often cited Benson as a role model, both for her strength and her compassion. Hargitay's influence on the industry can be seen in the increasing number of strong, complex female characters on television today, many of whom owe a debt to Hargitay's groundbreaking portrayal of Benson.

How Mariska Redefined the Role of Women in Television

Mariska Hargitay's role as Olivia Benson has had a profound impact on the way women are portrayed on television. When SVU premiered in 1999, female characters in crime dramas were often relegated to secondary roles, serving as love interests or supporting characters to their male counterparts. Hargitay's Benson broke this mold by being a fully developed character who was not defined by her relationships with men, but by her own strength, intelligence, and commitment to justice. In many ways, Hargitay redefined the role of women in television, showing that a female character could be both powerful and vulnerable, assertive and empathetic.

One of the most significant ways Hargitay redefined the role of women in television is through her portrayal of Benson's leadership. As the show progressed, Benson rose through the ranks, eventually becoming the Captain of the Special Victims Unit. This ascent to leadership was not just a plot point; it was a reflection of the growing recognition of women's capabilities in positions of authority. Benson's leadership was portrayed as strong yet compassionate, authoritative yet understanding. Hargitay's portrayal demonstrated that women could be effective leaders without sacrificing their humanity or their ability to connect with others.

Hargitay's Benson also broke new ground in terms of emotional complexity. In many crime dramas, female characters were often portrayed as either emotionally distant or overly emotional, with little nuance in between. Hargitay's Benson, however, was a character who could be both tough and emotionally available. Benson's empathy for victims, her personal struggles with her own traumatic past, and her determination to seek justice made her a relatable and multi-dimensional character. Hargitay's ability to convey this emotional depth set a new standard for female characters in television dramas.

Another way Hargitay redefined the role of women in television was through her advocacy for social justice. While SVU has always dealt with sensitive and important issues, Hargitay used her platform to push for more accurate and respectful portrayals of sexual violence and its impact on survivors. Her work with the Joyful Heart Foundation and her involvement in shaping SVU's storylines reflected a commitment to using television as a tool for social change. Hargitay's portrayal of Benson was not just about solving crimes; it was about raising awareness and giving a voice to those who had been silenced.

Through her portrayal of Olivia Benson, Mariska Hargitay redefined what it meant to be a woman on television. She showed that women could be strong, complex, and capable of leading, all while remaining empathetic and emotionally connected. Her performance has had a lasting impact on the industry and has paved the way for more diverse and nuanced portrayals of women in television. Hargitay's legacy as Olivia Benson will continue to inspire future generations of actresses, writers, and viewers, proving that the role of women in television is ever-evolving and full of possibilities.

CHAPTER 8

Overcoming Personal Challenges

Mariska Hargitay's career as Olivia Benson on Law & Order: SVU catapulted her into the spotlight, but alongside her professional success came numerous personal and physical challenges. Throughout her journey, Hargitay has dealt with significant obstacles, both emotional and physical, that have tested her resilience. However, each struggle has only strengthened her resolve, reinforcing her status as a role model both on and off the screen.

Physical and Emotional Struggles Throughout Her Career

The demands of portraying a character like Olivia Benson for more than two decades have been intense, requiring Hargitay to dig deep into emotionally draining material. As the show centers around cases of sexual assault, child abuse, and domestic violence, the emotional toll on

Hargitay has been significant. While she fully embraced the role, portraying the weight of these traumatic experiences week after week led to a great deal of personal reflection, and at times, emotional exhaustion.

Hargitay has been open about how difficult it can be to emotionally distance herself from the cases her character encounters. The harrowing storylines, many of which were inspired by real-life events, affected her profoundly, often requiring her to find ways to process the material in a healthy manner. It is no small feat to portray such emotionally intense situations while remaining compassionate and authentic. However, Hargitay found solace in knowing that her work had a purpose beyond entertainment—bringing awareness to the very real issue of sexual violence and giving a voice to survivors. This purpose drove her through the toughest moments, but she was always mindful of the importance of mental health and self-care.

Hargitay has credited her strong support system, including her husband Peter Hermann, for helping her navigate the emotional rigors of the show. Hermann's unwavering support provided her with stability, enabling her to continue channeling the intensity required for her role without becoming overwhelmed by the content. Still, balancing her demanding career with personal well-being has been an ongoing challenge throughout her life.

Injuries on Set and Recovery

While the emotional toll of SVU was considerable, Hargitay also faced significant physical challenges during her career. One of the most serious incidents occurred in 2008 while performing a stunt on the set of Law & Order: SVU. Hargitay was injured during a scene in which she was jumping through an exploding window. The stunt caused her to suffer a partially collapsed lung, a life-threatening condition that required immediate medical attention. Initially, Hargitay believed she had simply pulled a muscle, but the severity of her condition became clear as she struggled with intense pain.

After being diagnosed with the injury, Hargitay underwent surgery to repair the damage and was forced to take time off from filming to recover. Despite the seriousness of the injury, Hargitay demonstrated incredible resilience, returning to work just weeks after surgery. However, her lung issue recurred, and she needed a second surgery to fully resolve the condition. Even in the face of physical pain and the challenges of recovery, Hargitay's dedication to her craft remained evident. She didn't let the injury derail her commitment to SVU, instead embracing her recovery process with the same determination that has defined her career.

The injury, and the subsequent surgeries, were a wake-up call for Hargitay. She later reflected on how the incident forced her to reevaluate the way she approached her physical health and wellbeing. In an industry where actors often push themselves to the limit for the sake of their craft, Hargitay was reminded of the importance of setting boundaries and prioritizing her long-term health.

In interviews, Hargitay has been candid about the fact that her injury was a humbling experience that shifted her perspective on both her career and life. She used the incident as an opportunity to take stock of what was truly important to her—her health, her family, and her ability to continue advocating for others. The experience only deepened her resolve to continue making a difference through her work on SVU and beyond.

Personal Stories of Resilience and Overcoming Adversity

Hargitay's physical challenges are only part of the larger story of resilience that has defined her life. Throughout her journey, she has faced significant personal hardships that required inner strength and determination to overcome.

One of the most poignant examples of Hargitay's resilience can be traced back to the loss of her mother, Hollywood icon Jayne Mansfield, when Mariska was just three years old. Growing up without her mother and under the shadow of her fame was incredibly difficult for Hargitay. The trauma of losing a parent at such a young age is something she has carried with her throughout her life. Hargitay has spoken openly about how the loss of her mother shaped her perspective on life, teaching her the importance of cherishing family, finding strength in adversity, and using her experiences to build empathy for others.

Hargitay's journey of overcoming adversity didn't stop with the loss of her mother. The comparisons to Jayne Mansfield early in her career were often unkind, as Hargitay sought to carve out her own identity in Hollywood. Many people expected her to follow in her mother's bombshell image, and when she chose a different path, Hargitay faced skepticism. However, she remained focused on proving herself on her own terms, determined not to be pigeonholed or defined by her lineage.

CHAPTER 9

Beyond 'Law & Order: SVU' – Exploring Other Projects

While Mariska Hargitay has become synonymous with her role as Olivia Benson on Law & Order: SVU, her acting career and creative ambitions extend far beyond the boundaries of the long-running crime drama. Throughout her career, both before and during her time on SVU, Mariska has explored various film and television roles that highlight her versatility as an actress. She has also ventured into directing and producing, solidifying her influence in the industry and showcasing her talents behind the camera. This chapter explores Mariska Hargitay's projects outside of SVU, focusing on her work in film, television, and her forays into directing and producing.

Film and TV Roles Outside of 'SVU'

Mariska Hargitay's journey to becoming one of television's most recognizable stars began long before she took on the role of Olivia Benson. As the daughter of iconic actress Jayne Mansfield and former Mr. Universe Mickey Hargitay, Mariska was no stranger to Hollywood from an early age. Her career, however, was built on her own terms, and she worked diligently in a variety of roles across different genres, showcasing her talent long before Law & Order: SVU catapulted her to stardom.

Before landing her breakthrough role on SVU, Mariska appeared in numerous television shows and films. One of her earliest roles was in the 1985 horror-comedy Ghoulies, where she played Donna, a supporting character in a film about demonic creatures that wreak havoc on a group of young adults. Although it was a small part, it gave Hargitay her first taste of feature film acting. She also appeared in TV series such as Falcon Crest and Baywatch, where she gained experience in front of the camera and honed her acting skills.

Her versatility was further highlighted in guest roles on popular TV shows like Seinfeld, where she appeared in the 1993 episode "The Pilot," playing one of Jerry's potential love interests during the casting of a fictional sitcom. Her comedic timing and charm were evident, and it was clear that Mariska had a wide range of talents beyond dramatic roles. In fact, early in her career, she considered herself more suited for comedy and lighthearted parts, an interesting contrast to the gritty and serious role she would later embody as Olivia Benson.

Another notable role before SVU was her portrayal of Carly Fixx on the NBC drama ER in the late 1990s. In this recurring role, Mariska played a desk clerk in the busy Chicago emergency room. Though the role was relatively small, her appearances on ER helped solidify her as a talented actress capable of handling both drama and ensemble casts, a skill that would serve her well when she joined the cast of SVU.

Once she was cast as Olivia Benson in 1999, her career naturally became heavily associated with Law & Order: SVU. However, even during her time on the show,

Mariska managed to explore other acting opportunities. In 2001, she appeared in the romantic comedy Perfume, an ensemble film set in the world of the fashion industry. Although the film wasn't a major commercial success, it allowed Mariska to showcase a different side of her acting range, offering a lighter, more glamorous role compared to the intense, often emotionally heavy scenes in SVU.

Throughout her tenure on SVU, the demands of the show often limited her ability to take on extensive roles outside of it. However, Hargitay's dedication to acting and her love of storytelling were always present, and she often expressed her interest in pursuing more varied roles when time allowed. Her legacy as an actress is not confined to Olivia Benson, but rather as an artist who understands the nuances of human emotion, comedy, and drama, regardless of the role.

Directorial and Production Work

In addition to her accomplishments as an actress, Mariska Hargitay has proven herself to be a formidable force behind the camera. As her character Olivia Benson evolved on Law & Order: SVU, so did her role within the production team, as Hargitay took on new challenges as a director and producer. Her directorial debut came in the show's fifteenth season, and she quickly demonstrated that her talents extended far beyond acting.

Hargitay's first experience directing SVU was for the 2014 episode titled "Criminal Stories." This episode tackled difficult themes, including the media's portrayal of rape victims, and provided a perfect vehicle for Hargitay to bring her own sensibilities and experiences to the story. Known for her compassionate portrayal of Benson, Hargitay brought the same empathy to her directing, focusing on character development, pacing, and the emotional weight of the narrative. The episode received positive reviews, and critics praised Hargitay for her directorial choices, which gave the episode an intimate and urgent tone. Hargitay's seamless transition to directing marked a new chapter in her career, showing that she could tell stories not only from within the frame but also from behind the camera.

Following her debut, Hargitay continued to direct additional episodes of SVU, adding a distinct voice to the series. Her understanding of the show's complex characters, especially Benson, gave her a unique advantage as a director. She could coax emotional performances from her castmates because of her deep understanding of the material and her relationships with her fellow actors. Over time, Hargitay began to focus more on producing as well, taking on an executive producer role that allowed her greater creative control over the direction of SVU.

Her work as a producer and director also extended beyond SVU. Hargitay produced several advocacy-driven projects, including the critically acclaimed documentary I Am Evidence (2017), which explored the alarming backlog of untested rape kits in the United States. This documentary was a passion project for Hargitay, as it aligned with her work through the Joyful Heart Foundation, and it shed light on the systemic failures that prevent survivors of sexual violence from receiving justice. I Am Evidence went on to win a News &

Documentary Emmy Award, further cementing Hargitay's status as an impactful storyteller and activist.

Mariska's directorial and production work has allowed her to influence the kinds of stories that are told and how they are presented, making her an even more integral part of SVU and the broader conversation around justice and advocacy. By stepping behind the camera, she has ensured that the messages she cares about are not only conveyed on screen but are done so with the same level of care and integrity that she brings to her acting.

Other Creative Ventures

In addition to her directing and producing work, Mariska has explored various creative ventures that align with her values of advocacy and empowerment. While her schedule has always been demanding due to the rigors of filming SVU, she has expressed interest in expanding her work into new areas, including more film roles, advocacy-driven projects, and possibly even writing. Hargitay has spoken in interviews about her desire to tell more stories that resonate with audiences on a deeper level, stories that uplift and shed light on important issues.

Mariska's passion for advocacy and storytelling has also inspired her to mentor young actors and filmmakers, offering guidance and sharing her experiences in the industry. Her longevity in an industry known for its volatility speaks to her resilience, talent, and ability to adapt, and she continues to use her platform to support creative voices that might otherwise go unheard.

CHAPTER 10

Mariska's Lasting Legacy

Mariska Hargitay's impact on television and society is profound, transcending her role as Olivia Benson on Law & Order: SVU. Over more than two decades, she has become a symbol of strength, justice, and resilience, both on-screen and off. Her legacy goes beyond the critical acclaim for her portrayal of a detective fighting for victims of sexual violence—it also encompasses her advocacy work, her influence on real-world conversations about justice reform, and her embodiment of the values she has long fought for. This chapter explores the lasting legacy of Mariska Hargitay, examining how her career has shaped television, empowered survivors, and what her future holds.

The Impact of Her Career on Television and Society

Mariska Hargitay's portrayal of Olivia Benson stands as one of the most iconic characters in television history. Since Law & Order: SVU premiered in 1999, Hargitay has brought depth, humanity, and unflinching empathy to the role of a detective who fights tirelessly for victims of sexual violence. Unlike many procedural dramas that center around solving crimes, SVU has long focused on the emotional and psychological toll of these crimes on the victims, positioning Benson as their advocate and protector. This thematic focus has made the series a cultural touchstone, and Hargitay's portrayal of Benson has redefined how strong female characters are portrayed on television.

Hargitay's long-running role has also changed the landscape for female characters in television. When SVU began, the concept of a female lead in a crime procedural was still relatively rare, and Hargitay's character stood out for her complexity, compassion, and grit. Benson was not merely a sidekick or a love interest, nor was she portrayed as infallible. Hargitay imbued her with vulnerability, allowing viewers to see Benson's emotional struggles as she dealt with the trauma of the cases she encountered. Over time, this complexity not only endeared her to audiences but also helped challenge stereotypes about women in law enforcement and leadership roles on television.

The longevity of SVU is another testament to Hargitay's influence. Being the longest-running live-action prime-time series in American television history, SVU owes much of its success to Hargitay's dedication to the role. Her ability to evolve with the character, taking Benson from a young, driven detective to a seasoned captain of the Special Victims Unit, has kept audiences engaged. This evolution reflects not just the passage of time but also the deep connection Hargitay has with the character and the real-world issues SVU addresses.

The cultural impact of SVU is inextricably linked to Hargitay's portrayal of Benson. The show has brought issues of sexual violence, child abuse, and domestic violence into the mainstream conversation, raising awareness and challenging societal perceptions. The series has played a key role in educating viewers about the complexities of consent, trauma, and the legal system's treatment of survivors. Hargitay's portrayal of Benson as a fierce but empathetic advocate for victims has made her a symbol of hope for many who feel their stories are not being heard.

How Mariska Hargitay Became a Symbol of Strength and Justice

Beyond the television screen, Mariska Hargitay has become a symbol of strength, resilience, and justice in her own right. Through her activism, she has taken the values of her character and brought them into the real world. In 2004, she founded the Joyful Heart Foundation, a nonprofit organization dedicated to supporting survivors of sexual assault, domestic violence, and child abuse. The foundation's mission aligns closely with the themes explored in SVU, and Hargitay's passion for advocating on behalf of survivors is evident in her work. She has been instrumental in raising awareness about the backlog of untested rape kits in the United States, campaigning for policy reform and justice for survivors.

Hargitay's advocacy extends far beyond mere lip service. She has worked with lawmakers, law enforcement, and survivors themselves to push for justice reform. Her influence in this area has been profound, and her dedication has been recognized at the highest levels. Hargitay has testified before Congress, lobbied for legislation to address the backlog of rape kits, and used her platform to amplify the voices of survivors. Her activism has made her a role model for many, not just as an actor but as someone who is deeply committed to making the world a better place for those who have experienced trauma.

Her work has also changed the way society views sexual violence and its impact on survivors. Through both her role on SVU and her real-world advocacy, Hargitay has helped to dismantle myths surrounding sexual violence, such as the idea that survivors are to blame for their own victimization. She has consistently used her platform to empower survivors to speak out and seek justice, fostering an environment in which their stories are believed and respected. For many, Hargitay is not just an actress but a symbol of hope, embodying the qualities of strength, justice, and compassion that Olivia Benson represents on screen.

CONCLUSION

Mariska Hargitay's journey from aspiring actress to television icon is a story of resilience, talent, and a relentless commitment to making a difference both on and off the screen. Over the course of her illustrious career, she has transcended the boundaries of traditional Hollywood stardom, becoming not only a revered performer but also a powerful advocate for survivors of sexual violence and trauma. Through her portrayal of Olivia Benson on Law & Order: Special Victims Unit, Hargitay has become a symbol of strength, justice, and empathy, touching the lives of millions of viewers around the world.

Mariska Hargitay's portrayal of Olivia Benson is undeniably one of the most iconic roles in television history. Over two decades, she has evolved this character from a determined young detective into a wise, compassionate, and battle-tested leader, who not only seeks justice for survivors but embodies the emotional complexity and humanity of law enforcement officers who must navigate the darkest aspects of society. The role of Olivia Benson has become more than just a character on a television show—it is a symbol of hope and resilience for countless viewers, particularly survivors of sexual assault and abuse, who have found solace in Benson's unwavering pursuit of justice.

Hargitay's commitment to this role and her dedication to making Olivia Benson a fully realized, multi-dimensional character has earned her critical acclaim, numerous awards, and a place in the annals of television history. Her work has redefined the role of women in television, proving that female characters can be strong, vulnerable, and deeply human all at once. She has inspired a generation of actors, particularly women, who look to her as a trailblazer in the industry.

While Mariska Hargitay's influence on television is undeniable, her legacy as an advocate for change may be her most profound contribution. Her work with the Joyful Heart Foundation, which she founded in 2004, has made an immeasurable impact on the lives of survivors of sexual violence, domestic abuse, and child abuse.

Through the foundation, Mariska has raised awareness about the systemic issues that prevent survivors from receiving justice, particularly the backlog of untested rape kits in the United States, a cause she has championed tirelessly.

Her advocacy extends far beyond mere celebrity endorsement; she has become a leader in the fight for justice reform, using her platform to amplify the voices of survivors and push for legislative changes that protect victims and hold perpetrators accountable. Mariska's activism has earned her the admiration of countless individuals and organizations dedicated to social justice, further cementing her role as a change-maker in society.

Behind the camera, Mariska's personal life has been equally inspiring. Her ability to balance a demanding career with a strong commitment to her family speaks to her resilience and grace under pressure. Her marriage to actor Peter Hermann and their journey together as parents of three children demonstrate the importance of love, partnership, and finding balance in a life that is often defined by public scrutiny and professional challenges.

Throughout her career, Mariska has faced personal and physical struggles, including injuries sustained on set and the emotional toll of portraying such an intense character for over two decades. Yet, she has consistently demonstrated her strength and resilience, overcoming these challenges and using them as fuel for her work both on SVU and in her advocacy efforts.

In addition to her acting, Mariska's foray into directing and producing has solidified her status as a multifaceted creative force. Her work behind the camera on SVU and projects like I Am Evidence has allowed her to influence not just the stories that are told, but how they are told, ensuring that issues of justice, empathy, and survivor advocacy remain at the forefront. Her creative evolution from actress to director and producer is a testament to her desire to continuously challenge herself and expand her influence in the industry.

Law & Order: SVU stands as a cultural phenomenon that has reshaped the television landscape. Its longevity and relevance are, in no small part, due to Mariska Hargitay's leadership, both on-screen and behind the scenes. The show's exploration of sensitive topics such as sexual violence, trauma, and justice reform has sparked important conversations in society, offering a platform for the stories of survivors and shining a light on the challenges faced by law enforcement and victims alike.

Mariska's embodiment of Olivia Benson has left an indelible mark on popular culture, ensuring that SVU remains a vital and impactful part of the television world. The show's commitment to raising awareness about real-world issues, paired with Hargitay's advocacy work, has created a legacy that goes beyond entertainment—one that has influenced policy, inspired activism, and changed lives.

As Mariska Hargitay's career continues to evolve, her legacy as a groundbreaking actress, advocate, and director is firmly established. What comes next for Mariska remains to be seen, but one thing is certain: her impact on television, on survivors of trauma, and on society as a whole will be felt for generations to come.

In reflecting on her career and life, Mariska Hargitay once said, "Life begins at the end of your comfort zone." Indeed, it is this willingness to push boundaries, to step into uncomfortable spaces, and to speak out on behalf of those who cannot, that defines her legacy. Whether she is advocating for survivors, portraying one of television's most iconic characters, or raising awareness about critical social issues, Mariska Hargitay remains a force for good—a role model, an activist, and a true television icon.

Her story is not just one of fame and success, but of purpose and passion, leaving behind a legacy of compassion, justice, and strength that will continue to inspire for years to come.